Lee Canter's

Surviving Sibling Rivalry

Helping Brothers and Sisters Get Along

By Lee Canter and Marlene Canter

Lee Canter's

D1416579

Editorial Staff
Patricia Sarka
Barbara Schadlow
Marcia Shank
Kathy Winberry

Book Design
Bob Winberry

Cover Illustration
Patty Briles

© 1993 Lee Canter & Associates
P.O. Box 2113, Santa Monica, CA 90407-2113
800-262-4347   310-395-3221

Printed in the United States of America
First printing December 1993

99 98 97 96 95   10 9 8 7 6 5 4

ISBN 0-939007-77-0

"Mom, Kevin called me a jerk."

Dad, Billy's riding my bike again. Make him get off!

Why do I always have to take out the trash? You don't make Chris do anything!

"Did not!"

"Did!"

"Did not!"

"Did!"

"Did not!"

"Did! Did! Did!"

Sound familiar?

Are your children driving you crazy with their constant bickering and fighting? Do you dread even the shortest drives to the mall, knowing that your kids can't sit side-by-side in the back seat without some snide comment erupting into World War III? Are you tired of being the unappreciated and unwanted mediator in your children's squabbles?

You're not alone. Nearly every parent of two or more children is confronted with some form of sibling rivalry—from minor frays over sharing a toy to major ongoing battles.

Studies have shown that sibling rivalry is the cause of more stress, strain and concern among parents than any other parenting issue—other than discipline.

Parents Want to Know
Questions & Answers

Sibling rivalry is a common concern of every new generation of parents. Once the second child is born, situations arise and many parents need help coping with these very special problems.

Here are some common parent concerns:

Q As the single parent of three girls, I have difficulty trying to keep things fair. When my oldest girl needed a prom dress, the younger two pouted because they weren't treated to new dresses as well. I tried to explain, but all I got was the cold shoulder and a lot of guilt. Help!

Answer: Children can be very nit-picky when it comes to who gets what and how much. But the fact of the matter is that everything in life isn't fair and growing up with siblings teaches us this little life lesson early on.

Your children need some help with the definition of fairness. Fairness doesn't mean equal. Explain to your daughters that as a parent you give to each of them what you can based on their needs.

Q What is the best way to handle the jealousy our 3-year-old daughter has towards the new baby?

Answer: Almost all children are jealous to one degree or another when a new baby comes home. When a child has to make the transition from being the center of your attention to sharing the spotlight with a tiny, cuddly newcomer, you can expect some form of resentment. But there are steps you can take.

- Let your daughter help with the baby as much as possible. Make "bringing up baby" a team effort. There are lots of jobs to share: diapering, bathing the baby, folding clean baby clothes, "reading" a story while you are feeding the baby. While you are working together, rekindle stories of when she was a baby and how much easier it is now that you have such an able helper.

- Talk to relatives and friends. Explain that they should give equal time and attention to your daughter as well as the new baby. Suggest that if they are bringing gifts for the new baby that they remember your daughter with a special "something" as well (crayons, books, small toys).

- Give your daughter a new "doll baby" of her own. She'll love playing mommy to her doll while you are being mommy to the new baby.

- Relax your expectations during this time of transition. Many children revert to infantile behaviors (thumb sucking, wetting, baby talk) to get your attention. Be aware that this is normal.

- Remind your daughter how much you love her—all the time.

- Get a babysitter for the baby and spend special time with your daughter at least once a week. Go to the park, watch a movie, share a sundae. Devote all your time and attention to your daughter for a few hours and see her self-esteem soar.

- Visit your local bookstore or library. There are many storybooks available about adjusting to a new baby in the family—from a child's point of view. Read these together. Discuss your daughter's feelings about the new baby. Let her know through your words and deeds that your love for her has not been diminished at all by the new baby.

Q When my children get angry with one another, is it OK to let them punch dolls or toys instead of their brothers and sisters?

Answer: Allowing your children to act violently towards anything—animate or inanimate—is probably not the best alternative. Allow your children to express their angry feelings in other ways—with words, drawings, manipulatives.

- "I can see that you're angry with your sister. Can you draw me a picture of how you feel when she plays with your toys without asking?"

- "I can't allow you to hit your brother, but you can squeeze this clay as hard as you want."

- "You look like you need to let off some steam. For the next fifteen seconds you can yell 'I'm angry' as loud as you want."

Q As a working parent, I've got a perplexing problem. My eleven- and thirteen-year-old sons are home alone after school for two hours each day. At least once a day, I get a call from one son complaining about the other. Apparently they fight until I walk through the door. How can I make this arrangement work?

Answer: You need to establish some family rules about how you expect your sons to behave—when you are home and when you are at work. Be specific. If your sons are physically fighting when you're at work, make a rule about fighting. If your sons call each other hurtful names, outlaw name calling. If there are problems with sharing or privacy, make rules about these concerns, too.

Here is a sample list of family rules:

1. Don't hit, bite, pinch or kick.

2. Don't call each other names that are hurtful (such as stupid, fatso, ugly).

3. Knock before entering someone's bedroom.

4. Always ask permission before using someone else's toys, clothes or possessions.

These rules should be in force all the time. Explain that if your sons follow the rules and don't fight with one another, you will award them a point each day. When they have earned five points, you will reward their cooperative behavior with a special privilege (go to a movie, rent a movie or video game, eat out at a favorite restaurant). If, however, your sons choose not to follow the rules, you will be forced to remove privileges (such as phone and friend privileges).

Keep this in mind. Your sons may be fighting because they have nothing better to do. Schedule activities for your children to do when they come home. Ask that homework and chores be completed. Get your sons interested in hobbies. And, most importantly, praise your sons when they cooperate.

Why is sibling rivalry such a concern for parents?

There are many reasons why parents fret over their children's conflicts. If you think about your own situation you will probably relate to some or all of the following:

Sibling conflicts add stress to already stressful lives.
Battling brothers and sisters do not add harmony or peace to anyone's lives. A house filled with tension and arguments is not a pleasant place to return to at the end of a busy day.

When siblings constantly fight it's easy for parents to feel like failures—that they've done something wrong.
Many of us carry in our minds the picture of the "perfect" family where everyone gets along and goodwill abounds. When reality falls short of this image it's easy to blame ourselves—to feel that we are not living up to our parental responsibilities, or that we have done something to cause the problem.

Parents worry about underlying causes of anger and aggression.
When children fight, parents often worry that something serious is causing the conflicts. Divorced and separated parents often are concerned that their children have been adversely affected by family rifts. Working parents worry that they are not giving their children enough time. Single parents worry that their children are not growing up in an optimal family environment. Whatever the worries, the concerns they cause parents are very real.

Parents see sibling rivalry as destructive behavior that must be stopped.
For many parents, sibling conflicts are particularly frustrating because they think they should be able to stop them. When they aren't able to, the stress mounts.

Parents worry about the lasting effects of sibling rivalry.
Most parents hope that their children will share a life-long bond and be close to one another in adulthood. When children constantly fight, however, it's understandable that parents may feel this hope will never be realized.

Sibling conflict—it's a fact of most families' lives.

First of all, relax. Although it's easy for battle-weary parents to believe that the sibling conflicts they experience are a problem restricted to their own family, the truth is that fighting between brothers and sisters is a normal and inevitable part of life in any family with more than one child.

Think back to your own childhood. If you have a brother or sister, the chances are pretty good that you also had plenty of battles. The chances are also pretty good that you came through these battles none the worse for wear. (Your parents may have been frazzled, but you were probably fine.)

It's important to understand that sibling rivalry is normal and doesn't usually lead to any long-term damage. It's just as important, however, to realize that there are steps you can take to minimize the problems that do come up.

The goal of this book is to give you a plan for surviving sibling rivalry—realistic answers that will help you cope with the day-to-day stress and aggravation it causes.

But before addressing those issues, let's look at some of the reasons why siblings fight in the first place.

Why Siblings Fight

I don't care <u>why</u> they fight, I just want them to stop!

You may think it doesn't matter *why* your children fight, but knowing some of the reasons may help you to both cope with the stress of the moment and minimize the fighting in the future.

The "whys" of sibling conflicts can be looked at in two ways: the *lightweight* (and most common) reasons for fighting and *major* reasons for fighting.

Lightweight Reasons for Fighting

Not every fight your children have is about something of major importance. Not every fight means something disturbing is going on or your child is upset over some injustice, imagined or real. Siblings will fight, period. Here are some of the more typical reasons children fight.

Siblings fight simply because they are siblings.
Whenever you have more than one child, conflicts are inevitable. The closer in age, the greater the likelihood of ongoing sibling rifts. When children are six or more years apart, however, there are generally fewer problems.

Siblings fight because they enjoy it.
Sometimes children fight simply because it's fun. They like needling each other. They like getting on one another's nerves. Within the comfort and security of the family, siblings can indulge in arguments and vent their feelings without fear of losing face or friends.

Siblings fight because they have nothing better to do.
Do your children fight as much when they are completely engrossed in a pleasurable activity? Probably not. When they're bored, however, watch the skirmishes skyrocket! (Remember those long car rides punctuated by pokes, shoves and disparaging remarks? That's boredom at work.)

The next time you worry over what in the world might be causing your children to fight, remember that the *majority* of sibling conflicts are due to these very reasons. Knowing this may help you keep things in a more reasonable perspective, and worry and concern to a minimum.

Major Reasons for Fighting

Some sibling conflict is, of course, generated by real feelings that your child is dealing with as a natural course of growing up. It is helpful to be aware of these reasons because often there is something you can do to lessen the severity of or even avoid the conflicts they generate.

Siblings fight because they are competing for parental attention.
Children often feel that they must compete with brothers and sisters for their parents' approval, love and attention. This is particularly common when feelings of jealousy arise over the arrival of a new baby, and can often be seen when a parent

is very involved in the activities of one child, such as coaching the soccer team or planning a birthday party.

Siblings fight because they are unable to share.

Children are expected to share lots of things: toys, the television, the telephone, a bedroom, the backyard and even friends and acquaintances. Sharing is not easy for most children. Among siblings, where feelings of jealousy and envy are also present, it's even harder.

Siblings fight because they are concerned about fairness.

"It's not fair! You always take her side!"

Every parent has heard this lament countless times. Children are keenly attuned to gauging whether or not a parent is treating each one equally. Their internal calculators seem to keep a running tally of compliments given, time spent, money handed out, and privileges awarded.

Knowing some of the causes of sibling conflict can help parents look at problems in a more understanding light. No, it's still not OK to hit your sister or brother because you want the telephone, but it's important for parents to recognize the feelings that may generate these conflicts and to understand that sibling rivalry is natural and not limited to your household or caused by your own shortcomings.

In fact, once you understand some of the origins of sibling conflict, you may be able to take a deep breath and see that these battles aren't all bad for your children.

Sibling conflicts serve a purpose.

As irritating as sibling conflicts are, parents need to know that these ongoing battles actually serve a purpose in a child's growth and development. They create opportunities for children to learn how to cope with real-life conflicts. They give children practice in dealing with and resolving problems within the security and forgiving atmosphere of the home.

For example, through sibling conflict children learn:

1. how to negotiate.
2. how to share.
3. how to deal with feelings of envy and resentment.
4. how to solve problems with words.

Think about this . . .

If you look at the conflicts your own children have had, you will see that as these conflicts are worked through and resolved your children have gained experience in all these skills. These experiences will serve your child well as he or she learns to function outside the family.

Although some sibling battles are inevitable, the good news for parents is that you have daily opportunities to prevent or reduce many of these conflicts. The rest of this book will give you guidelines to follow that will help you deal most effectively with sibling conflicts—things you can do to anticipate and minimize problems, and steps you can take once problems occur.

Part 1 Creating a Positive Family Environment

The day-to-day environment within your home has a great effect on how all family members, including siblings, treat each other and get along. While you cannot expect to eradicate all sibling conflicts, they will most likely be less severe and cause less stress when children live and grow within a positive family environment.

A positive family environment is a place where each person counts, and where each person can count on one another. In such an environment, children learn the rules by which they will live the rest of their lives. They learn self-esteem (how they feel about themselves) and self-control. They learn to be responsible and respectful. In such an environment the family provides children with opportunities to grow to be the best that they can be— through good health and proper nutrition, education and love.

Parents can ensure a more positive family environment by doing the following:

1. Model the behaviors you want your children to develop.
2. Have family rules and set limits to back up those rules.
3. Catch your children being good—and praise them!
4. Take time every day to make each child feel special.

Model the behaviors you want your children to develop.

Many of the habits parents find most annoying in their children are habits children have learned by watching the adults in their lives.

- Children of battling spouses learn that fighting is an acceptable way to handle problems.
- Children who are physically punished by parents learn that it's all right to hit those you love.
- Children who hear parents call one another derogatory names learn that putdowns are perfectly OK.

Become a positive role model.
Each day you have new opportunities to model and teach positive behaviors and to instill in your children a positive outlook on life. The example parents set is powerful. From the time children are babies they will absorb and learn the attitude and the values that you project.

What kind of a person do you want your child to be? What values do you want to promote in your children?

Children can learn kindness, consideration, empathy, cooperation, patience, fairness, tolerance, understanding, appreciation, thoughtfulness and positive communication from the way we as parents relate to others in our lives.

Children can learn to see the "glass as half full, not half empty" from the way their parents embrace life. They learn self-confidence and independence from the way we meet the challenges of daily living.

Children can learn to say "Thank you" and "Please," "May I" and "I'm sorry" when these are woven into the fabric of family communication.

Smiles, hugs, encouraging words and unconditional love should be the legacies we give our children every day of our lives because these are the most precious of family heirlooms passed from one generation to another.

The values you embrace and demonstrate will affect they way your children treat each other.

A positive family environment will not end sibling conflicts, but such an environ-ment *will* increase the likelihood that your children will treat each other with respect and caring.

This poem by Dorothy Law Nolte shows how we as parents can posi-tively (and negatively) affect our children's lives with our words and actions.

If children live with criticism,
    they learn to condemn.
If children live with hostility,
    they learn to fight.
If children live with ridicule,
    they learn to be shy.
If children live with shame,
    they learn to feel guilty.
If children live with tolerance,
    they learn to be patient.
If children live with encouragement,
    they learn confidence.
If children live with praise,
    they learn to appreciate.
If children live with fairness,
    they learn justice.
If children live with security,
    they learn to have faith.
If children live with approval,
    they learn to like themselves.
If children live with acceptance
    and friendship,
They learn to find love in the world.

Establish family rules.

As parents you have the right to expect everyone in the house (and that includes siblings, too) to show respect and common courtesy to each other—and to follow some basic rules. Family rules are the standards you set for acceptable —and unacceptable—behavior in your household.

Think about your own family. Are there spoken (or unspoken) rules about the right way and the wrong way to behave? Do your children know how you feel about fighting, name-calling, the right to privacy? If your children are aware of your family rules, good for you. Communicating how you want children to behave is very important. If you only "think" your children know how they should behave, then it's time to create a list of family rules and share them at a family meeting.

Rules really *are* OK with children.
Contrary to what many parents think, children actually do like to have a fair set of rules to live by. Living in a house without rules can be very frustrating. It's not fair when behavior that's ignored one day (for example, calling your sister a "stupid idiot" for forgetting to deliver a phone message) results in punishment the next time it occurs.

Your children may not like the rules you set, but if they are sure that you will enforce them consistently and fairly, they will probably respect them.
Keep these guidelines in mind when creating your set of family rules:

Choose rules that will help minimize problems between siblings.
Here's your opportunity to go on the offensive in minimizing sibling battles. If physical fighting is an ongoing problem in your home, make a rule about fighting. If name-calling is a constant source of irritation, outlaw it. Everyone in a family has the right to live without the threat of physical harm or verbal abuse. If it takes rules to enforce these unwritten laws, then write them.

Make rules specific.
Your rules will be easier to comply with and enforce if they are specific. Vague rules such as "Don't treat your brother unkindly" or "Always be nice" can lead to confusion. What a parent considers as "unkind" or "nice" behavior may be defined quite differently by a seven-year-old. Be as specific as possible. If little Bobby is a biter, outlaw biting. If fifth-grader Frank is a whiz at personal attacks and ego-damaging putdowns, place name-calling on your list of no-no's. If twelve-year-old Twyla goes closet-hopping every morning without permission, stop her in her tracks with a rule about borrowing.

Keep rules simple.
No lengthy paragraphs, please. A simple sentence for each rule will do.

Limit family rules to five or less.

Too many rules may be hard for your little ones to remember. And with five rules, you can use the "one-hand method" of reviewing the rules. As you point to each finger on your hand, recite the rule.

Note: It's very important not to include rules that you know realistically can't be followed all the time. For example, unless it is exceedingly important to you, and a real, consistent problem, a rule such as "No yelling or shouting" is probably going to cause bigger problems than it's worth. Everyone shouts and yells at one time or another, making this rule difficult to enforce.

Here's a sample Family Rules Chart. Note that the rules are simple and specific.

Family Rules

1. Don't hit, bite, pinch, or kick others.
2. Don't call each other names that are hurtful.
3. Knock before entering someone's bedroom.
4. Ask permission before using someone else's toys.

Note to Parents: Make sure that the rules apply to everyone.

Don't expect your children to abide by family rules that you do not plan to follow, too. If the rule is no hitting, then no one should be physically abusive—to anyone. No spousal shoving matches. No spankings for unruly children. If the rule is no name-calling, then parents must follow suit—with children and spouses alike. The behavior you model is the behavior your children will ultimately emulate.

Explain the rules at a family meeting.

Once the rules are chosen, write them on the **Family Rules Chart** (see page 39). Then gather the family together for a special meeting. Discuss each rule and talk about why it's important.

"In our family we all have the right to be treated with courtesy and respect. To help us keep this in mind, even when we get upset, we are going to have some family rules."

Post the Family Rules Chart in a prominent place—on the refrigerator, a bulletin board, or perhaps framed and hung on the family-room wall. The chart will serve as a constant reminder of how everyone in the family should behave toward one another.

Catch Your Children Being Good—and Praise Them!

Experts agree that many sibling squabbles are started just to get a parent's attention. Children want and need our attention—and sometimes they'll do whatever they have to do to get it. If Mom ignores Susie when she's playing peacefully with her little brother, a quick shove will have brother crying and Mom running to see what all the fuss is about.

A parent's dilemma is deciding when to give attention and when not to. The key, however, is to give plenty of attention for good behavior.

These guidelines will help you decide when to run and when to stay put:

- **Don't give a child a great deal of attention for misbehaviors.**
  That's like throwing gasoline on a fire! If you want to extinguish unacceptable behavior, don't fuel it with your attention. If it's a minor squabble you may want to ignore it. If the misbehavior requires your intervention, however, do it as simply and quickly as possible. No lengthy discussions or question-and-answer periods.

"Cary, that's the second time you've walked into your sister's room without knocking first. Go to your own room now for ten minutes."

No further discussion.
No further attention.

- **<u>Do</u> give your children attention when they do behave.**

  This is the secret ingredient to increased family harmony! Give your children special attention when they are *not* fighting, bickering or bothering one another. A smile, a pat on the back, or a few words of praise and encouragement send a gentle "thumbs up" message. And by praising their good behavior, your children will be more likely to repeat the behavior in order to get that much-desired attention again.

"Thank you for taking turns with the new video game."

"That was nice of you to share your doll clothes with your little sister."

"I like the way you two are playing the Chutes and Ladders game."

"Two heads are better than one. You put that puzzle together in record time."

Encourage sibling cooperation.

Motivate your children to cooperate with one another—and then catch them being good—by setting up a Cooperation Station. Your children will soon get the message that just by getting along with one another they can earn special privileges—rent a video, have friends spend the night, a picnic in the park.

You'll need:
- a piggy bank, shoebox, or covered container
- pennies, tokens (game chips, slips of paper)
- Cooperation Station Chart (see page 41)

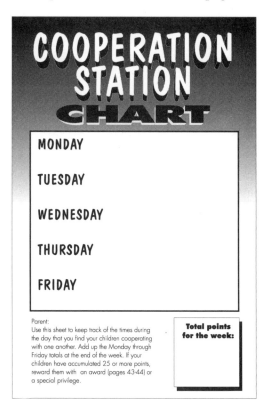

COOPERATION STATION CHART

MONDAY

TUESDAY

WEDNESDAY

THURSDAY

FRIDAY

Parent:
Use this sheet to keep track of the times during the day that you find your children cooperating with one another. Add up the Monday through Friday totals at the end of the week. If your children have accumulated 25 or more points, reward them with an award (pages 43-44) or a special privilege.

Total points for the week:

- Colossal Cooperation Award
  (see pages 43-44)

COLOSSAL COOPERATION AWARD

Congratulations are in order for

_____

Names

Because you have made this week so special by cooperating with one another, you are hereby awarded

_____

_____

_____

_____

_____

_____

Parent Signature

_____

Date

Here's how it works:

- Label the piggy bank (or any container) with the words "Cooperation Station."

- Explain to your children that whenever you catch them cooperating, you will drop a penny into the piggybank (or a token into a container). **Note**: Don't forget to praise them for their good behavior while you're depositing the penny.

- Explain that at the end of the day, the pennies (or tokens) will be counted. If the children have collected a minimum of 5 (or any number) pennies, they will receive a special prize or privilege (popcorn snack, stay up an extra 10 minutes, relaxing backrub, etc.)

- Keep a tally of the daily numbers on the Cooperation Chart (see page 41).

- On Friday, count up all the numbers for the entire week. If they have accumulated a total of 25 (or any number) of points, give your child a **Colossal Cooperation Award** (see pages 43-44). On the award, write down an extra special prize or privilege your children have earned for their week's worth of colossal cooperation.

Take time every day to make each child feel special.

Your children want and need your individual attention. Set aside 10 to 15 minutes each day to devote special one-on-one time to each of your children. This time should be away from others in the family. When the baby is taking a nap, play a game or read a book or talk about the day with an older child. Bedtime is the perfect opportunity to spend special time with each child. In fact, your children will come to anticipate these bedtime sessions —and you can send them off to sleep knowing that they are unique and special in your eyes.

Special one-on-one activities:

- Read a favorite book.
- Tell an amusing story about a special event in your child's life.
- Take a walk together.
- Play a game.
- Assemble a puzzle or build with blocks.
- Sing a song and record it on a cassette.
- Browse through a magazine or catalogue together.
- Write a letter together to a faraway friend or relative.
- Work on a craft project together.
- Cook a special treat together.
- Plant some seeds.
- Wash the dog; brush the cat; teach the parakeet to talk.
- Exercise together.

A positive family environment has an impact not only on sibling conflicts but on all of your family interactions. A home filled with mutual respect and consideration is a home in which children can grow, flourish and become responsible, caring adults. The responsibility of parents is to provide such an environment. The benefit is a home freer of conflicts and richer in caring, compassion and love.

Part
2 Preventing Sibling Conflicts

As has been pointed out, sibling conflicts are inevitable and, in fact, your children will learn some important life lessons as they maneuver their way through them. But that does not mean that battling children are pleasant to be around or that you should have to accept it all of the time. Savvy parents take steps to both minimize and prevent problems by doing the following:

1. Check for patterns in their children's fights.
2. Anticipate problems and plan for them.
3. Give specific directions for special situations.

Check for patterns in your children's fights.

Do your children seem to fight more in the morning? Just before dinner? At bedtime? When friends visit? When playing games or watching TV?

By looking for patterns in your children's behavior, you can more effectively plan to get past these problems or, in some cases, avoid them altogether.

Here's what to do:

Chart your children's fights for a few days. Jot down the time each fight begins and the activity they were engaged in. You will probably find that certain activities and certain times of the day are more conducive to rifts between siblings. Just having this information may give you ideas for heading them off.

There are usually some relatively simple solutions to these types of "patterned" fights.

For example:

PROBLEM: Children fight <u>every after-noon</u> for control of the television.

Brother #1   It's my turn to pick the show today. You got to choose the show yesterday!

Brother #2   No, it isn't! We had to watch that stupid ninja movie the day before and that was two hours long.

Brother #1   So what, it's still my turn."

Brother #2   No, it's not. Give me that remote!"

SOLUTION: Make a "Things We Share" Schedule. If you allow your children to watch a half-hour of TV after school and an hour of TV after dinner, alternate choices. Let one child choose the afternoon programs for one day while the other child chooses the evening programs. The next day have your children exchange times. Record this information on an inexpensive wall calendar. Award your children a star on the calendar for each day they follow the schedule and cooperate. When they have accumulated five stars, take them out to "share" a treat!

20

PROBLEM:	Children get cranky and fight with one another every afternoon about a half-hour before dinner.
Preschooler:	That's my toy! Give it back.
Toddler:	(holds onto toy tightly and begins swatting at older child)
Preschooler:	(hitting back and grabbing at toy) Give it to me. I want it.
Toddler:	(begins kicking and screaming, but still has firm grasp on toy)
Preschooler:	(finally wrestles toy from toddler, but in the process falls back, hits head on wall, and starts screaming)
Toddler:	(starts wailing because he's lost control of the toy)

SOLUTION: They are probably hungry, so feed them. Children use up a lot of energy during the day, and waiting until dinnertime to refuel may be just too long of a wait. (Adults can get cranky when they're hungry, so why not kids?) Try feeding your young ones a healthy snack in the afternoon or, if possible, feed them their dinner early. This may be just the recipe for an afternoon of cooperation rather than aggravation.

PROBLEM:	Children fight over household chores.
Brother:	I fed the cat yesterday, so it's your turn today.
Sister:	No it isn't because I fed her for two days in a row before that. So it's your turn again.
Brother:	That's not fair!
Sister:	Well, it's not fair for me either and I'm not going to do it.
Brother:	Well, neither am I!

SOLUTION: Create a Chores Chart.
Be very specific about your children's household job responsibilities. Make a list of the jobs that must be completed during the week and assign specific jobs to each child. If feeding the cat is a household responsibility, assign it to your daughter for an entire week while assigning taking out the trash to your son. Sharing job responsibilities offers many opportunities for problem situations.

By noticing patterns in your children's conflicts, and using a little ingenuity, you will find that some difficulties can be avoided altogether.

Anticipate problems and plan for them.

Many sibling conflicts are predictable, and you know from past experiences when they are likely to erupt.

Listen to your intuition. If you hear a voice telling you, "I think we're going to have a problem if," then make plans to bypass the problem with some common-sense planning.

For example:

SITUATION: Your oldest daughter is having a slumber party. She'll probably receive lots of attention from her guests.

Anticipate the problem:
Her younger sister wants attention, too. She may try to get it by bothering the girls at the slumber party.

Possible solutions:
Give your younger child the attention she needs by spending one-on-one time with her **during** the party. If her favorite snack is chocolate chip cookies, whip up a batch together while the party is going on and let your daughter have her "moment in the spotlight" as she passes out some of the cookies at the slumber party.

Here's another example:

SITUATION: You're leaving the children with a new babysitter for the evening. Your seven-year-old daughter is very concerned about fairness. Your six-year-old is very competitive and manipulative.

Anticipate the problem:
If the children play a competitive game (such as Candyland or Chutes and Ladders) you'll probably have problems.

Possible solutions:
Meet with your daughters before the babysitter arrives to decide on videos or programs to watch, toys to play with, or books they would like read to them. Schedule some separate activities, too. Steer your daughters away from competitive games that might cause arguments. Offer them an incentive to cooperate. Have the babysitter place a star on the Cooperation Station chart (see page 41) each time they cooperate and behave during an activity. If they receive a predetermined number of stars, they earn a special privilege for their good behavior.

Give specific directions for special situations.

Specific directions are different from the Family Rules (see page 14) you have in place all of the time. These directions cover how you expect your children to behave during different situations. This is especially important when sibling fights could cause safety problems.

Read through the list below and check off the situations during which your children tend to argue and fight. Then decide how you need your children to behave to ensure their safety and your sanity.

Siblings need to behave better when they are:

☐ in the car

☐ at the market or mall

☐ at the doctor's office

☐ at the home of a relative or family friend

☐ at home when family friends are visiting

☐ at home when playmates are visiting

☐ at holiday gatherings and annual family events

☐ at restaurants

☐ at school functions (play, conference, sporting event)

☐ at church or synagogue

Your directions should be simple and observable.

For example:

When we are in the car:
1. Sit in your assigned seat with seatbelt fastened.
2. No yelling.
3. Keep hands and feet to yourself.

Note: Always plan for the "boredom factor." Remember children tend to bicker and fight when they have nothing better to do, so plan activities when appropriate. An "on the go" kit containing toys, books, cassettes, and snacks will help keep brother and sister from fighting.

When we are at the market:
1. (younger children) Stay seated in shopping cart. (older children) Walk next to shopping cart.
2. Keep hands off items on shelf.
3. No whining or begging for certain foods or items.
4. Keep hands and feet to yourself.

When we are eating a meal:
1. Keep hands and feet to yourself.
2. Eat without playing with your food.
3. No fighting with siblings or teasing.
4. Ask permission to leave the table when finished.
5. Place dirty dishes in sink.

Often children do not behave properly simply because they haven't clearly been told what to do. Keep in mind that children want to please. They want to do what's right, but to do so they need to know exactly what your expectations are.

1. **Look for patterns** in your children's conflicts.

2. **Anticipate problems** before they begin, and have a plan for avoiding them.

3. **Give specific directions** for different situations.

By following these three guidelines you will be able to prevent, or lessen the severity of, many sibling battles. And that means far fewer headaches for you.

3 What to Do When Your Children Fight

In spite of all your preventive efforts, your children *will* fight. What you do, or don't do, about those fights can spell the difference between your own frayed nerves and how your children respond to your actions.

In this part of the book we will first look at how you can best handle minor squabbles. Then we will see what you can do when problems escalate.

How to Handle Minor Squabbles

Minor squabbles are those daily annoying interactions that can drive you crazy but in and of themselves probably don't mean a lot. Often the best way to handle these minor conflicts is to just let them go. These are the times when children will learn how to solve problems on their own.

Here are some pointers for handling these beginning-stage squabbles:

Tune out minor bickering.
When your children start bickering, take a deep breath and remind yourself that *your* children don't hold the monopoly on sibling squabbles. Remind yourself that most siblings fight and they fight a lot. Sometimes it's easier to put up with your children's minor spats when you know that most other parents have to endure the same kinds of daily aggravations with their children as you do.

Put some space between you and your children if their minor squabbles are too distracting. Find some peace and quiet in another section of the house. There's nothing like the muffled sounds of clothes tumbling in the dryer, the hum of a lawnmower, or the melodic tones of a favorite record to erase the annoying sounds of bickering children.

Resist the urge to mediate your children's minor battles.
If your children get into the habit of relying on you to step in and solve their problems, they will never learn how to work things out for themselves through cooperation and compromise. When your children come crying or complaining to you, turn the problem back to them and let them know that they have to figure the problem out by themselves.

Follow these guidelines:

First, acknowledge their anger and their problem:

> "I can see that both of you are very angry. You want to watch one program and you want to watch something else."

Then let them know you are confident that they can work it out.

> "I'm sure that you two can come up with a solution that will be fair to both of you."

If appropriate, remind your children of the Family Rules and/or special directions for the activity they are engaged in.
If necessary, give your children and warning—and a choice.

For example:

If your children are annoying each other while playing together, take 15 seconds to remind them of the rules for play.

"Remember our rules in this house: Keep hands and feet to yourself. If you cannot follow these rules, I will have to give you both a ten-minute time out away from these toys. It's your choice. Play together without yelling or shoving or lose the privilege of playing with these toys."

Don't encourage tattling.

Children in the midst of a minor squabble often want to drag a parent into the middle of the fray by tattling. This is the kind of behavior you don't want to encourage by giving it much attention. When the tattler approaches you with his/her complaints, give a noncommittal nod and make a simple statement of fact:

"It's too bad you children are not getting along."

Don't reproach. Barely respond. Remember, unless you have seen a problem first hand, you will not likely gain an accurate picture just hearing it reported by your child.

When Problems Escalate

When your children's bickering and arguing snowballs from a minor squabble to a more serious fight it's time to step in and take action.

You need to step in:
- when fighting becomes physical.
- when verbal attacks become personally hurtful and ego-damaging.
- when the situation becomes uncomfortable or unbearable.
- when you are at your wit's end and find yourself losing control. (You've had it.)
- When you need peace and quiet in the home.

You need to take action by:
- separating the children, and
- following through with your warnings by giving consequences.

Here's what to do:

First, take command of the situation.
It's time to pull in the reins and stop this fight. Your words and actions should convey that you have to intervene because of your children's inability to make better choices about their behavior.

Describe the trouble in non-judgmental terms and explain what will be done to stop the fight and why. Depending upon the severity of the situation, you may wish at this point to clearly and firmly warn your children that they have a choice: they must either end the fight <u>immediately</u> or they will be separated and (depending on the situation) face loss of certain privileges.

"I see Jason slamming the bedroom door and Jerry calling him names. This noise is unacceptable, and no one in this house has the right to call anyone else hurtful names. Your fighting about television again is interfering with our family. No one can read, talk on the phone or talk with each other because your fighting interferes.

"Consider this a warning. If you two can't resolve your differences right now I'll have to step in and take further action. You both have a choice. Stop fighting or you will be choosing to spend the evening in separate rooms and lose TV privileges for the rest of the night."

If the fighting continues, take action.
If problems continue, your first action should be to separate your children. After all, they can't fight if they're not within striking (or speaking) distance. Give your children time-outs in separate areas. Separate bedrooms are perfect time-out stations, but if this isn't possible, seat the fighting children on chairs in separate, uncrowded areas of the house.

This time away from each other may defuse the anger that fanned the flames leading to the fight. It also provides quiet time for your children to reflect on the conflict and perhaps come up with some better behavior choices.

Say to your children:

"I've given you the opportunity to resolve this by yourselves, but I can see that you are unable to get along tonight without fighting. Jerry, into the bedroom. Jason, into the den."

Finally, follow through with logical consequences.
If you promised to remove certain privileges if the fighting continued, follow through. In many sibling conflicts, logical consequences are the most effective way to let your children know that you mean business. Logical consequences are the removal of privileges that relate to the conflict.

Here are examples of conflicts and corresponding logical consequences:

Conflict	Logical Consequence
Fighting over TV	Loss of TV privileges
Fighting over the phone	Loss of phone privileges
Fighting over a toy	The toy is put away for a certain time
Taking another's possessions	Sibling's room is off limits
Fighting over video games	Games are taken away

"You weren't able to figure out how to resolve your arguments about the TV, so the TV is off limits for the rest of the night. I know there was a movie you both wanted to see, but remember, this is a choice you made."

Remember, if you fail to back up your warnings with actions, your words will be meaningless and you will have lost all power to control the situation—this time and in the future.

4 How to Resolve Continuing Problems

Some sibling problems are chronic—they just don't go away no matter what preventive actions you take. If you are dealing with an ongoing problem, it's time to try something different. The following two ideas have proven effective in many households:

1. Hold a family problem-solving meeting.

2. Use a Sibling Contract.

Hold a Family Problem-Solving Meeting.

A family meeting between parent(s) and children is often a productive way to sort out a persistent or difficult problem and find a workable solution. This meeting shouldn't be a forum for gripes and complaints, but an exchange of ideas—with everyone sharing their concerns and suggestions. Older children particularly will appreciate the opportunity to speak out and be heard. Younger children may need help articulating their concerns, but the process is just as beneficial for them.

Follow these guidelines for conducting a family problem-solving meeting:

Let each child talk about the problem and explain how it's affecting him or her.

It's important that each child has an opportunity to air personal concerns. Give them their "day in court," but insist that conversations be calm and polite, with no interruptions allowed. Explain that each child will have a chance to speak.

For example:

Parent: We have an ongoing problem between Jan and Meg that is making everyone unhappy. We're holding this family meeting to see if we can come up with some ideas that will solve the problem and make everyone's life more pleasant. First, let's talk about what the problem is. Jan, would you start please?

Jan: Meg is always borrowing my stuff without my permission. Yesterday she took my new markers to color her paper and then left the tops off the markers so now they're all dried up. She does this with everything of mine. I hate sharing a room with her. I can't stand it anymore.

Parent: Meg? You know that one of our family rules is to respect the property of others. How do you feel about this?

Meg: I wasn't going to keep the markers. I just needed to use them for a little while. Then Jan yelled at me and grabbed the markers out of my hand. She even tore the paper I was coloring. She's so selfish; I hate her! She never shares anything with me. I don't ask because she'll just say no.

Ask each child what he or she wants to happen.

Parent: Jan, what would you like to see happen about this problem?

Jan: I just want her to leave all my stuff alone. My things don't belong to her. If she needs something she can ask me first. I'll decide whether or not she uses them.

Parent: Meg? What would you like to happen?

Meg: I want her to stop yelling at me all the time. I share my things with her and I don't see why she can't share with me. Sometimes I need to use something of hers. Sometimes it's important.

Summarize the conversation to this point. Let your children know what you perceive to be the problem.

Parent: OK. Jan, I hear you saying that you don't want Meg to borrow things without asking. And Meg, you are saying that you don't want Jan to yell at you, and you think she should share. Any ideas about how we can make this happen?

Have everyone brainstorm ideas for solving the problem.

Listen carefully and don't dismiss any suggestions. Write suggestions down for later discussion. When the brainstorming is finished, read the list aloud. Ask each child what solutions he or she is comfortable with.

Parent: OK. You both have made lots of suggestions. Now I'd like each of you to suggest something you are willing to do to help solve this problem. Meg, what do you think?

Meg: I'll ask Jan permission before I use any of her stuff. If I return anything broken or wrecked, I will replace it out of my allowance. But I want Jan to help me out sometimes, too.

Parent: Jan?

Jan: If she asks first, I'll try to
         lend things sometimes. But
         just because she asks
         doesn't mean that I have to
         give it to her.

**Make sure everyone understands
what he or she is going to do. Plan
to meet in the near future to see how
things are working out.**

Parent: Meg, you've agreed to ask
         permission before taking any
         of your sister's things. And
         Jan, you've agreed to help
         out by sometimes lending
         Meg something she needs to
         use. Let's meet again in one
         week and see how this is
         working out.

Be sure to have that follow-up meeting,
whether the situation has improved or not.
If problems have decreased let your
children know how proud you are of
them. If problems persist, you may want
to try another solution that was suggested
in your meeting.

> Keep in mind that a problem-solving
> meeting will do more than tackle an
> immediate problem. It also teaches your
> child important life skills, to verbalize
> feelings and to communicate in a
> productive manner.

For a different strategy for resolving
continuing problems, you may want to try
a Sibling Contract (pages 45-46).

If Problems Persist . . .

If the actions you have taken to minimize sibling conflicts have not been successful, and you find yourself caught in a power struggle with your children, it's time to use the **Sibling Contract** (see page 45).

What is a Sibling Contract?

This contract is a written agreement between you and your children that states:

- the new **rule** the children must follow,

- the specific **reward** your children will receive when they follow the rule.

- the specific **consequences** that will be provided if your children chooses not to follow the new rule.

Rules

Meet with your children to discuss the specific problem. Explain that together you will develop a new rule in the house. Depending on the specific problem your children are having with each other, the new rule may be:

___ No teasing.
___ No tattling.
___ Do not take another's possessions without asking first.
___ No name-calling. (Be specific.)
___ Do not interrupt one another while on the phone (when friends are visiting, etc.).
___ Other_____

Say to your children, for example:

"The two of you been having too many problems lately, and these problems are usually because of name calling. This is upsetting us all, and it has to stop. It's not OK in this house to hurt each other's feelings like this. To help both of you learn to think before you speak, we are going to have a new household rule. The new rule is 'no name calling.'"

Write the new rule on the Sibling Contract (pages 45-46).

Rewards

Decide how you will reward your children for following the rule. The best way to motivate your children to get along with one another is to use the Cooperation Station (see pages 17 and 18.) Set a daily and weekly goal that both children can work toward. Your children can earn:

__ P.S. I Love You Coupons.
__ An evening at the library or another "night out" with the family.
__ The rental of a special video movie or game.
__ Special time with parent on an individual basis.
__ Other _____

Say to your children, for example:

"I know you can treat each other with more kindness and more consideration. Here's what I'm going to do to let you know how much I appreciate it when you do treat each other in this way.

Each day that there is no name calling at all I will put 5 tokens in the Cooperation Station. When you earn 15 tokens we will all go out together to a movie."

Write the reward on the Sibling Contract (pages 45-46).

Consequences

Decide what privilege or activity you will take away if your children do not choose to follow the new rule. For example, your children might:

__ Be sent to separate parts of the house to cool off.
__ Lose the privilege of playing games together for a specified time period.
__ Lose the privilege of participating in a family outing.
__ Lose TV or phone privileges.
__ Not be allowed to play with the toy or game in question for a specified period of time.
__ Other _____

Say to your child, for example:

"I hope you'll be successful and earn those tokens, but if there is any more name calling I will have to take a privilege away. If I hear either of you calling the other a name, that person will lose the right to watch TV the rest of the day."

Write the consequence on the Sibling Contract (pages 45-46).

Sign it and date it.

Once the contract is completed, sign and date it. Then post it on a cupboard, bulletin board or the refrigerator door.

SIBLING
CONTRACT

The new rule in our house will be:

No name calling.
New Rule

If   *Chris and Terry*
Name(s)

follow the rule,

each day there is no name calling
Reward
you will earn 5 tokens.

If   *Chris and Terry*
Name(s)

don't follow the rule,

-you will lose the privilege of
Consequence
watching TV the rest of the day.

_____
Parent's Signature

_____
Children's Signature

_____
Date

Remember, you must be consistent.

• If your children break the rule, you must follow through with the consequence.

• If your children follow the rule, you must provide the reward.

• Praise your children often whenever you catch them following the rule.

How to Speak So Your Children Will Listen

> I can talk till I'm blue in the face but they still don't listen!

Do your children tune you out, ignore you, or argue with you when you ask them to cooperate, share, or stop bickering and fighting? If this is commonplace in your home it may have a lot to do with the way *you* are speaking to your children.

Parents who are successful in encouraging better behavior speak to their children in a clear, direct and firm manner that leaves no doubt about what is expected.

Parents who are ignored or argued with often speak in a way that is either wishy washy or hostile.

Do any of these comments sound familiar?

"How many times do I have to ask you two to share your toys?"

"Won't you *please* try and get along together?"

"This is the fourth time today I've had to speak with you about your fighting."

"Why can't you treat each other like you care?"

Chances are you've said things like these to your children many times. Most parents have. But what do statements like these really say? Look at each one carefully and you will see that they either ask pointless questions, beg, or make an obvious statement of fact. In any case, they do *not* tell the children what you want them to do. They do not let children know without a doubt that you expect their behavior to change. Wishy-washy statements don't let your children know that your words are to be taken seriously—that you mean business.

They make it easy for your children to ignore you.

And what about comments like these?

"I should know better than to expect you two to act like mature children."

"I've had it. If this fighting keeps up both of you are going to be sorry."

"That's it. You're both grounded for two weeks."

What do these all-too-common remarks say to children? Put-downs, meaningless threats and off-the-wall punishments, because they are emotional and often inappropriate, are an invitation to challenge and anger. Because they disregard a child's feelings they send a message to the child that says, "I don't like you." Hostile responses tear down a child's self-esteem and are ultimately damaging. The words your children hear from you will become the way they feel about themselves.

Learn to speak so your children will listen.

Don't beg. Don't get angry. Don't become exasperated. Instead, when making a request of your children, be calm and use direct statements that send this message: "This is what I expect you to do."

"Lisa and Maria, your arguing has gone too far. I want you to turn off the TV now."

"Mario and Rosa, I want each of you to go to your own bedrooms now."

"Rob and Sara, turn off the video game and put it away."

Confident, clear and direct statements get results.

And if your children argue?

Above all, don't argue back. Do not get involved in a discussion. It will get you nowhere. The following scene illustrates this point:

Parent: Kathryn and Paul, I'm tired of hearing you argue about the phone. It's off limits for the rest of the evening.

Kathryn: Why do I have to be punished? It's Paul who kept grabbing it.

Paul: It's not fair. She's been on it over an hour. This always happens and it's not my fault.

Parent: I'm sorry if it's not fair but how can I tell who's in the right and who's in the wrong?

Paul: Well, if you can't tell, why do I have to be punished? I need to call Leo about our homework assignment.

Parent: Why? Didn't you write your assignments down? I'm really tired of this, Paul.

Paul: I just forgot. It's no big deal.

Kathryn: Mom, please, just one short call to Amanda? Then I'll stay off. I have to tell her something important.

Parent: It's always important with you. Fine, you can each make one call, but make them short.

What happened here? By arguing—by getting into a pointless discussion—the parent has lost control of the situation. Now she's addressing issues that have nothing to do with the phone, and the arguing hasn't stopped. And the children are still using the phone.

What should you do in a situation like this?

Use the "broken record" technique. First, very clearly tell your child what you want him to do. If he argues, simply repeat the statement, like a broken record. Do not argue back or even discuss the issue. *Repeat your expectation.*

For example:

Parent: Kathryn and Paul, I'm tired of hearing you argue about the phone. It's off limits for the rest of the evening.

Kathryn: Why do I have to be punished? It's Paul who kept grabbing it.

Paul: It's not fair. She's been on it over an hour. This always happens and it's not my fault.

Parent: I understand that you want to use the phone, too, but the phone is off limits for the rest of the evening.

Paul: I need to call Leo about our homework assignment. Am I supposed to miss my work just because Kathryn messed up?

Kathryn: And I need to talk to Sara.

Parent: I understand that you both are upset because you want to use the phone, but the phone is off limits.

Paul: You're being so unfair. I just need the phone for a few minutes. It's important.

Parent: The phone is off limits. Period.

By staying firm, not arguing, not getting sidetracked, chances are good your children will comply with your request. They may grumble and complain, but they will probably get up and do as asked.

If necessary, back up your words with actions.

If, however, after three repetitions of your expectations your children still do not comply, it's time to back up your words with actions and present your children with a clear choice:

Parent: Paul and Kathryn, hang up the phone now. If you choose to continue to argue both of you will choose to lose phone privileges tonight and tomorrow too. The choice is yours.

By giving your children a choice you place responsibility for what happens right where it belongs—squarely on your children's shoulders.

Try these techniques the next time your children ignore your requests or argue with you. Just take a deep breath and follow through calmly and confidently. You'll find that this approach *does* work!

Pages 39 - 46 contain the worksheets that were introduced in this book. Two or more copies of most worksheets are provided. You may want to make additional copies before using so there will always be an ample supply on hand.

Family Rules

Family Rules

(blank lined writing space)

COOPERATION STATION CHART

MONDAY	
TUESDAY	
WEDNESDAY	
THURSDAY	
FRIDAY	

Parent:
Use this sheet to keep track of the times during the day that you find your children cooperating with one another. Add up the Monday through Friday totals at the end of the week. If your children have accumulated 25 or more points, reward them with an award (pages 43-44) or a special privilege.

Total points for the week:

COOPERATION STATION CHART

MONDAY

TUESDAY

WEDNESDAY

THURSDAY

FRIDAY

Parent:
Use this sheet to keep track of the times during the day that you find your children cooperating with one another. Add up the Monday through Friday totals at the end of the week. If your children have accumulated 25 or more points, reward them with an award (pages 43-44) or a special privilege.

Total points for the week:

COLOSSAL
COOPERATION
AWARD

Congratulations are in order for

_____

Names

Because you have made this week so special by cooperating with one another, you are hereby awarded

_____

_____

_____

_____

_____

_____

Parent Signature

_____

Date

COLOSSAL
COOPERATION
AWARD

Congratulations are in order for

Names

Because you have made this week so special by cooperating with one another, you are hereby awarded

_____

_____

_____

_____

_____

_____
Parent Signature

_____
Date

SIBLING
CONTRACT

The new rule in our house will be:

_____
New Rule

If _____
Name(s)

follow the rule,

_____
Reward

_____

If _____
Name(s)

don't follow the rule,

_____
Consequence

_____

_____
Parent's Signature

_____
Children's Signature

_____
Date

SIBLING
CONTRACT

The new rule in our house will be:

_____
New Rule

If _____
Name(s)

follow the rule,

_____
Reward

_____

If _____
Name(s)

don't follow the rule,

_____
Consequence

_____

_____
Parent's Signature

_____
Children's Signature

_____
Date

Lee Canter's
Top 10 "Sibling Rivalry" Reminders

The guidelines presented in this book will help you both put sibling conflict into perspective and take steps to minimize the problems it causes you and your family. Here are some thoughts to keep in mind as you continue to navigate the turbulent waters of parenthood.

1 First and foremost, relax. Sibling conflict is a fact of life you share with parents of any family that has more than one child. Conflict between brothers and sisters is an absolutely natural, absolutely normal part of growing up. If your children fight it doesn't mean you've done something wrong or that they have severe problems. It simply means they're growing up—together.

2 Keep in mind that sibling conflicts serve a purpose. When your children fight they are learning how to negotiate, how to share, how to deal with feelings of envy and resentment, and how to solve problems with words. These are important skills they will need throughout their lives. What better place to learn these skills than in the home?

3 Be a positive model. Children learn behaviors they see demonstrated in their own lives. If you don't want to hear your children yell at each other—don't yell. If you don't want your children to hurl verbal putdowns to each other, select your own words carefully. Set an example of how people treat one another through your own relationships. Show your children how a caring person behaves towards others.

4 Maintain family rules that stress consideration and respect. Rules provide guidelines that will help your children choose behaviors that are most important.

5 Praise good behavior! When your children treat each other respectfully and show that they care for one another let them know how much you appreciate it. Your praise, more than anything else, will motivate them to choose positive behavior. An especially good time to offer praise is when your children successfully resolve a conflict on their own.

6   Pay attention to what your children are fighting about. Although many sibling conflicts are inevitable, there are things you can do to ward off or avoid some of the more predictable and annoying problems.

7   Stay out of their fights! One of the most common mistakes parents make in dealing with sibling problems is to get involved too often and too prematurely. If a parent always steps in at the first sign of conflict children will never learn how to resolve problems on their own. Unless your children have really crossed the line: physical or verbal assaults (or you've just plain heard enough) let them work things out for awhile.

Give them the opportunity to negotiate, to solve problems with words and to deal with their feelings.

8   Some sibling problems just aren't solved easily, and sometimes you will have to step in to resolve ongoing conflicts. Keep in mind that it's to your benefit, and your children's, to actively help them make better behavior choices. A sibling contract (as described in this book) will give you the structure you sometimes need to get your children on track.

9   An argument with one child can be frustrating enough. When two are involved it can send tempers skyrocketing! All the more reason to speak so your children will listen. When your children don't cooperate with your requests don't argue and don't beg for compliance. Stay firm. Calmly state your expectations, and repeat them if necessary. Don't get involved in pointless arguments or defensive discussions. In a heated three-way altercation someone has to keep a cool head and stay focused.

10 Listen to your children's concerns. Sometimes they may need to air their differences in the nonjudgmental, caring environment of a family meeting. This meeting *shouldn't* be a gripe session or a tattling contest. Instead, it is an opportunity for you and your children to problem solve together. The message to your children will be that in your family everyone is taken seriously, and you will work together to arrive at mutually beneficial solutions.